Dentistry in the Scriptures

Compiled by Philip M. Hudson
(with editorial comments)

Copyright 2020 by Philip M. Hudson.

Published 2020.

Printed in the United States of America.

All rights reserved.

No portion of this book may be reproduced, stored in a retrieval system, or transmitted in any form or by any means – electronic, mechanical, photocopy, recording, scanning, or other – except for brief quotations in critical reviews or articles, without the prior written permission of the author.

ISBN 978-1-950647-56-9

Illustrations – Google Images.

This book may be ordered from online bookstores.

Publishing Services by BookCrafters
Parker, Colorado.
www.bookcrafters.net

Table of Contents

Introduction..i
Dentistry in The Scriptures...1
Author's Note..253

Appendix One..271
About The Author...281
By The Author..283

Introduction

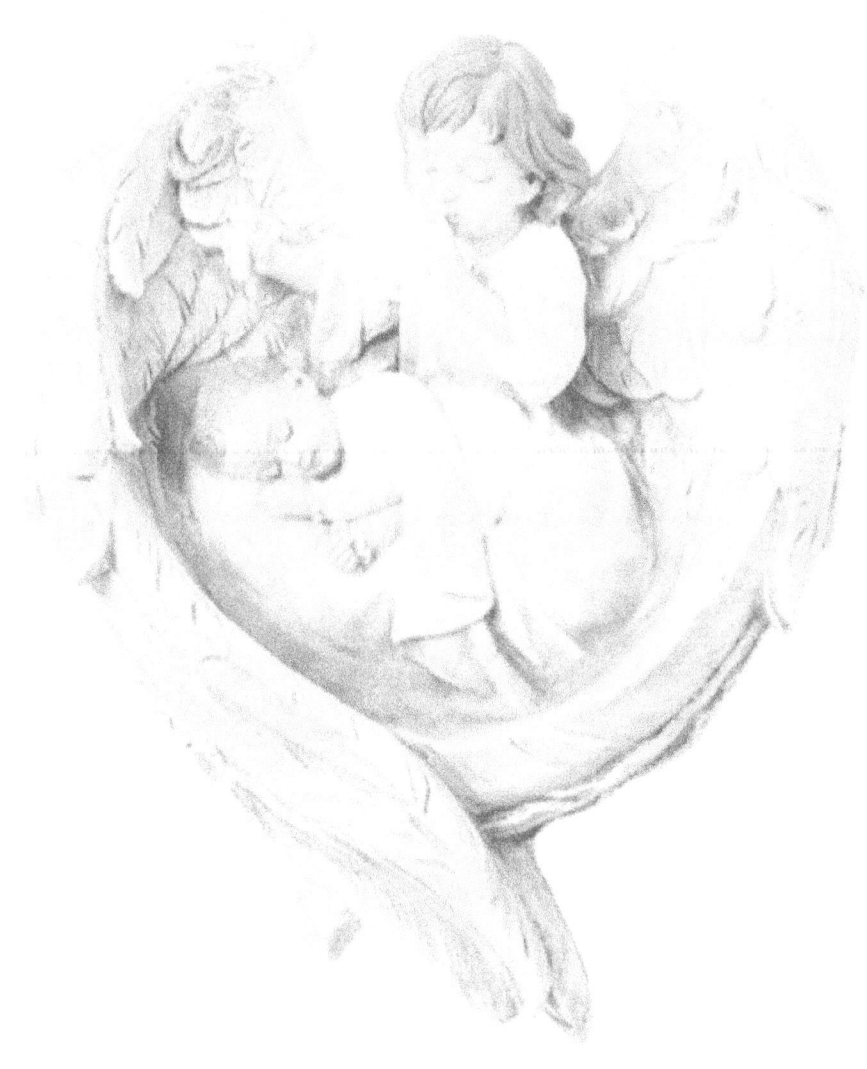

It is quite amazing how many references there are to dentistry (+/- 125) in the holy scriptures. By comparison, "doctor" is mentioned 3 times, just one-tenth as often as lowly "dung." "Medicine" is mentioned just 4 times, trumped by "soothsayers" (9 times), "vomit" (10 times), and "wizards" (12 times). "Health" pales in comparison to "sickness," (19 times versus 97 times).

Any and all variations on "Universal Health Care" are conspicuously absent in the scriptures. It is reasonable to conclude that medical care was elusive in ancient Israel, while oral health care was not only esteemed by the people, but was also easily accessible to them.

One hundred twenty five references to dentistry in the scriptures.

From the beginning of time, there has been an interest in esthetic dentistry. It was with hopeful anticipation that Jacob envisioned the outcome of Judah' cosmetic teeth lightening: "His eyes shall be red with wine, and his teeth white with milk." (Genesis 49:12).

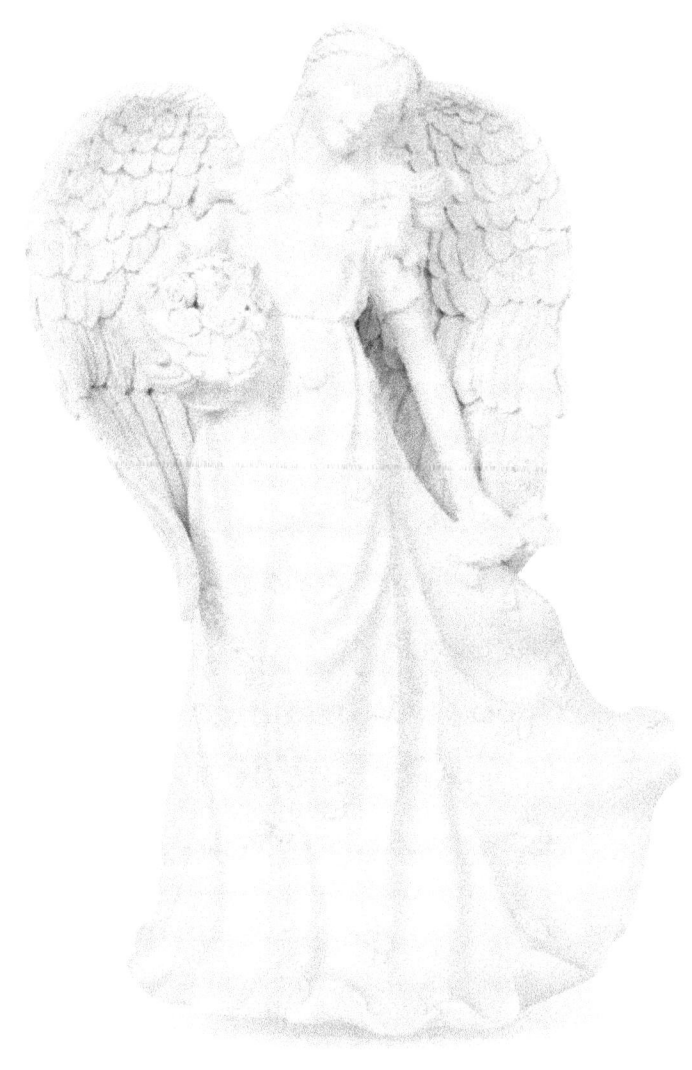

Speech can be difficult after the administration of local anesthetic. On one such occasion, Moses complained "to the Lord, I am slow of speech, and of a slow tongue." (Exodus 4:10).

Early on, Moses was interested in oral anatomy, posing the question: "Who hath made man's mouth?" (Exodus 4:11).

After reviewing a busy appointment schedule, an Israelite receptionist reassured one anxious patient: "In the morning, ye shall be filled." (Exodus 16:12).

Autogenous transplants
were only then being perfected.
"Eye for eye, tooth for tooth,"
wrote Moses. (Exodus 21:24).
Today we might instead
offer an implant.

In the Old
Testament, we read how one
dentist went to great lengths to
protect a tooth, with a beautiful
crown. Moses observed how "he
overlaid it with pure gold
within and without, and
made a crown of gold
to it, round about."
(Exodus 37:2).

To avoid damage from the blistering hot sun of the Megev Desert, the precaution was given to one patient to "put a covering upon his upper lip." (Leviticus 35:14). Preferably, an aloe vera salve.

We have all witnessed a social gaffe, similar to that which was recorded by Moses: "The flesh was yet between their teeth, ere it was chewed." (Numbers 11:33).

There is mention made in the Old Testament of surgical endodontics: "But God clave an hollow place that was in the jaw." (Judges 15:19).

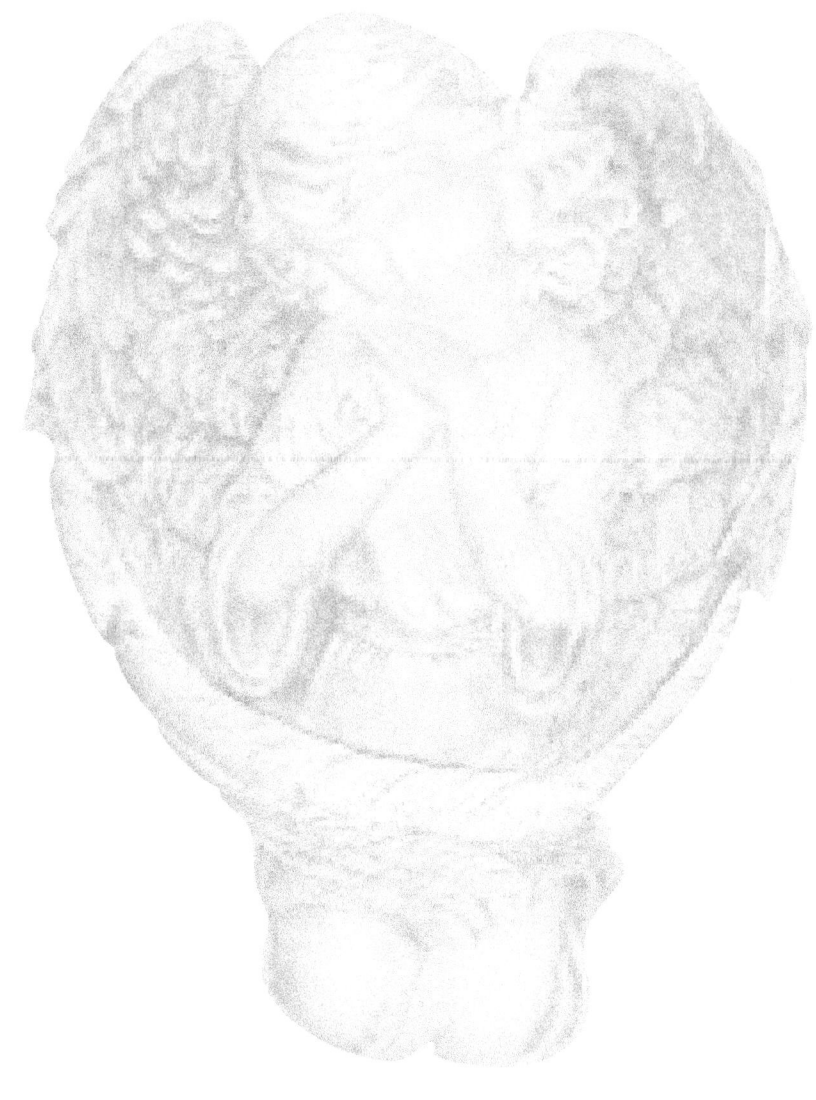

On at least one occasion in Israel, after a particularly intense course of Botox, a dentist negatively reported of a patient that "her lips moved, but her voice was not heard." (1 Samuel 1:13).

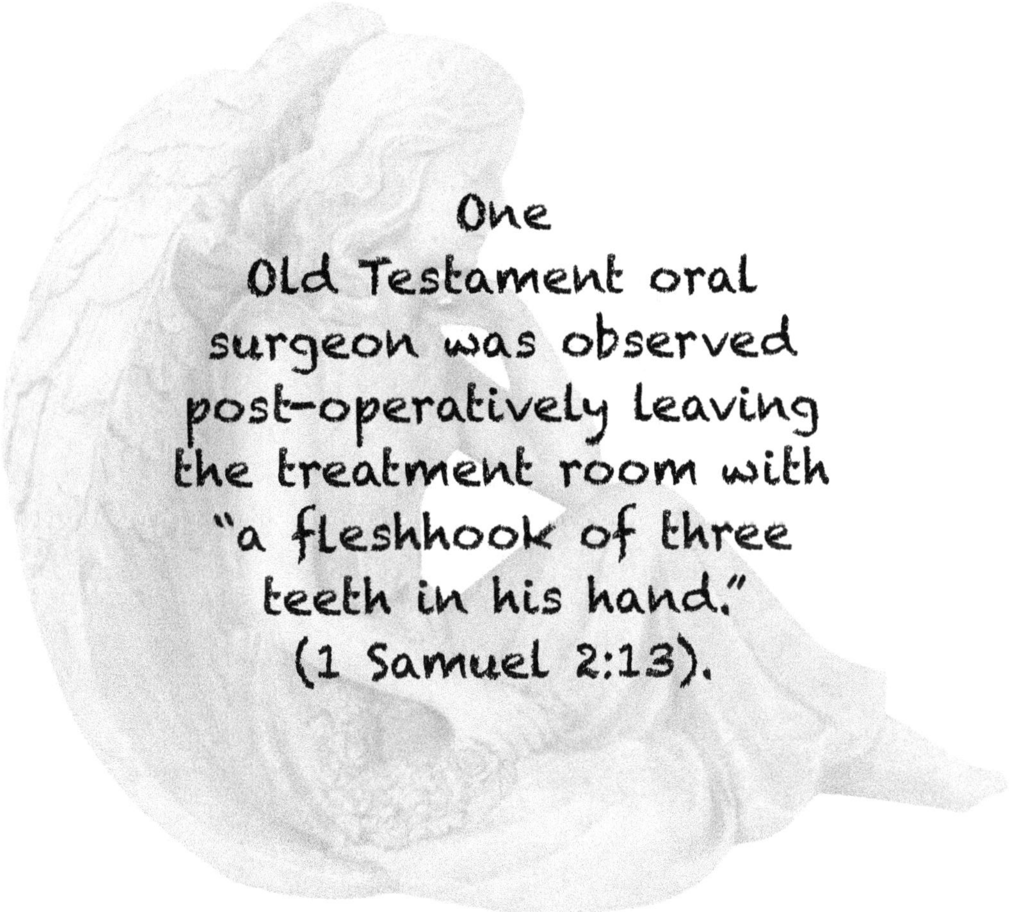

One
Old Testament oral
surgeon was observed
post-operatively leaving
the treatment room with
"a fleshhook of three
teeth in his hand."
(1 Samuel 2:13).

When
Samuel heard
the voice of the Lord
in the temple, it was as
"fire out of his mouth" that
was as a "blast of the breath
of his nostrils," reminscent of
some of the patients dentists
saw, from time to time.
(2 Samuel 22:9 & 16).

After visiting the royal dentist, "Mordecai went out from the presence of the king ... with a great crown of gold." (Esther 8:15).

Stress can cause
the rapid build up of
pathogenc oral bacteria.
Such a condition prompted
Job to exhort the children of
Israel to take a chill pill,
that they might "be hid
from the scourge
of the tongue."
(Job 5:21).

Without the benefit of modern era antibiotics, soft tissue infection and suppuration were problems. "Is there iniquity in my tongue?" Job asked his dentist. "Cannot my taste discern perverse things?" (Job 6:30).

As Job reflected, we all need to floss better. "Wherefore, do I take my flesh in my teeth?" he asked. (Job 13:14).

Speech therapists encouraged their patients to follow their example: "I would strengthen you with my mouth, and the moving of my lips." (Job 16:5).

Job uncomfortably reported of one acquaintance: "He gnashed upon me with his teeth." (Job 16:9).

Job admitted he had a halitosis problem, sighing: "My breath is corrupt." (Job 17:1).

Who
among us hasn't
shared the experience
of Job, who, describing one
confrontation with adversity,
disclosed: "I am escaped with
the skin of my teeth."
(Job 19:7).

There were
limits to what
a dentist could do.
One patient came home
after an appointment, only
to report: "My breath is
strange to my wife."
(Job 19:17).

Reconstructive
surgery wouldn't be
possible until the Last Days. In
the meantime, it was reported of
some with congenital defects that
"their tongue cleaved to the
roof of their mouth."
(Job 29:10).

Job described how oral and maxillo-facial surgery harmonized with restorative dentistry in Old Testament times: "I brake the jaws of the wicked, and plucked the spoil out of his teeth." (Job 29:17).

"Canst thou put an hook into his nose, or bore his jaw through with a thorn?" Job asked, when he brought a friend to his dentist for a new patient consultation. (Job 41:2).

After performing an exam, one Israelite dentist recorded her terse asssessment on a patient's chart: "His teeth are terrible round about." (Job 41:14).

The Psalmist praised the Almighty, that He had "broken the teeth of the ungodly" who had evidently forgotten to wear their mouthguards during physical confrontations with Deity. (Psalms 3:7).

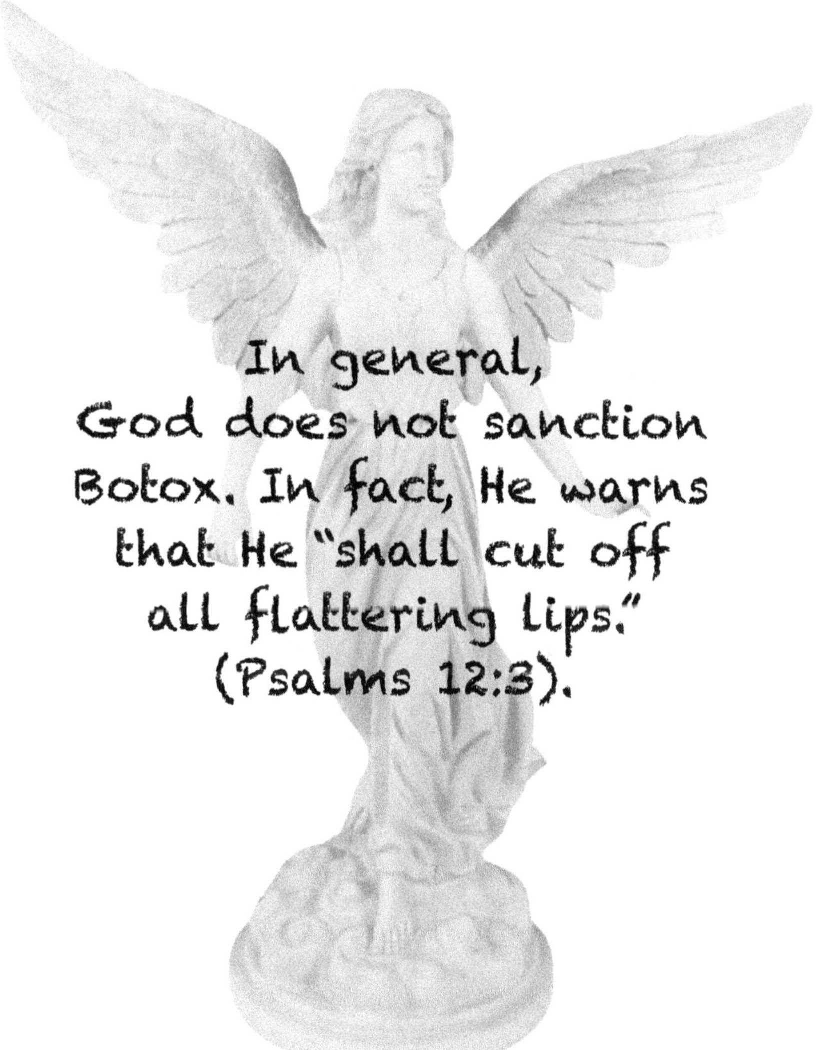

In general,
God does not sanction
Botox. In fact, He warns
that He "shall cut off
all flattering lips."
(Psalms 12:3).

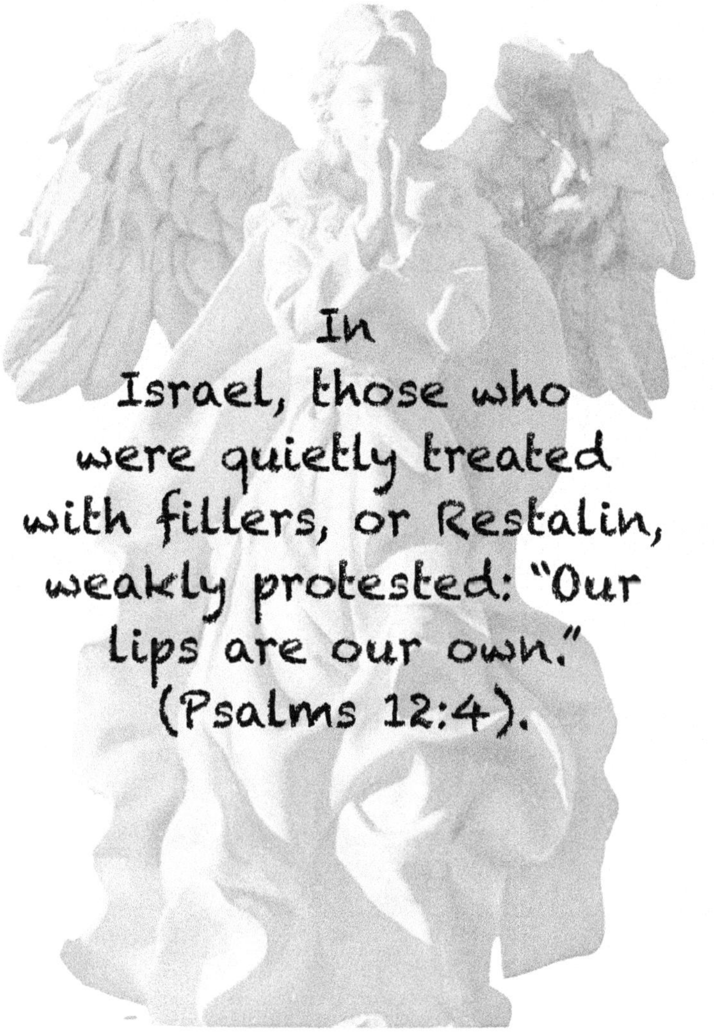

In
Israel, those who
were quietly treated
with fillers, or Restalin,
weakly protested: "Our
lips are our own."
(Psalms 12:4).

Describing an anatomical anomaly, the Psalmist wrote: "My tongue cleaveth to my jaws." (Psalms 22:15).

David lamented of his enemies: "They gnashed upon me with their teeth." (Psalms 35:16).

Bracketing the teeth with orthodontic appliances was not universally accepted in Israel. One innovative young man who declined conventional care, determined instead: "I will keep my mouth with a bridle." (Psalms 39:1).

The
mouth can be an
armory that houses
weapons of war. David
cried: "I lie even among
them that are set on fire, even
the sons of men, whose teeth are
spears and arrows, and their
tongue a sharp sword."
(Psalms 57:4).

We are reminded of the frenzy of World Wide Wrestling, when, from the scriptures, we hear David shout: "Break their teeth, O God, in their mouth." (Psalms 58:6).

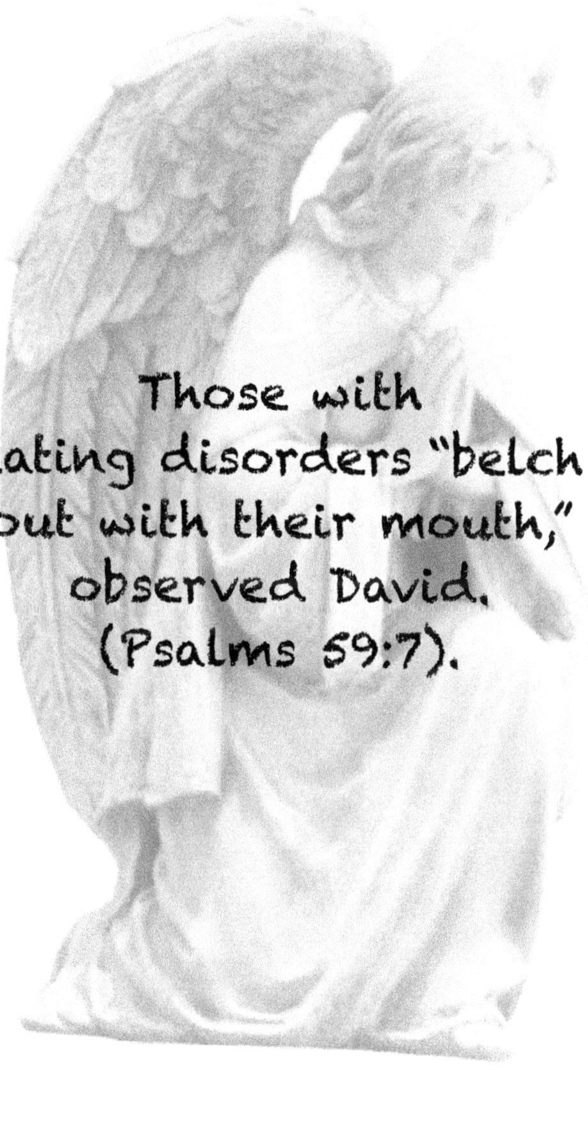

Those with
eating disorders "belch
out with their mouth,"
observed David.
(Psalms 59:7).

In spite of vocal opposition from some who complained: "Thou hast profaned his crown by casting it," the best way to fabricate a gold restoration was still by the lost-wax technique. (Psalms 89:39).

Communication has always enjoyed a dependent relationship with the dentition. Long ago, David observed of those in Israel who neglected their oral health: "They have mouths, but they speak not."
(Psalms 115:5).

Would an ethical oral surgeon disfigure a patient, as did some in Israel? David divulged how "they have sharpened their tongues like a serpent." (Psalms 140:3).

When we practice proper
oral hygiene, the result can
be spectacular: "For the lips of
a strange woman drop as an
honeycomb, and her mouth
is smoother than oil."
(Proverbs 5:3).

When the available financial resources of his subjects were squandered on wine, women, and song, to the neglect of oral health care, King Solomon was moved to declare: "The mouth of the foolish is near destruction." (Proverbs 10:14).

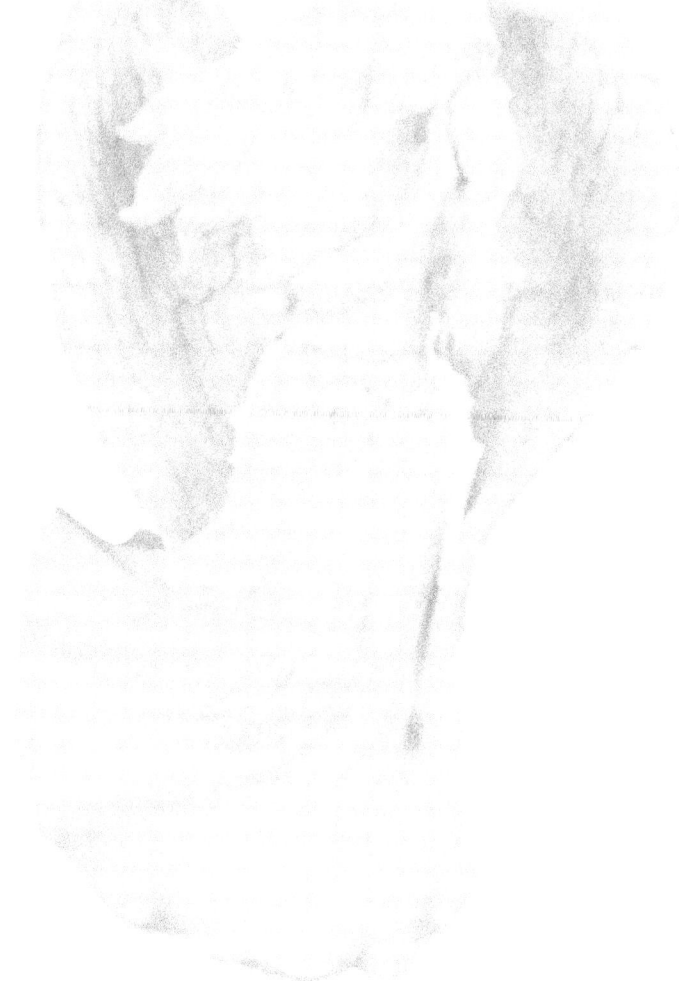

Solomon decried bizare Israelite health care philosophies, as well as their practitioners, saying: "As vinegar to the teeth, and as smoke to the eyes, so is the sluggard to them that send him." (Proverbs 10:26).

"The froward tongue shall be cut out." Ouch! (Proverbs 10:31).

As they say, garbage in, garbage out. "He that keepeth his mouth keepeth his life; but he that openeth wide his lips shall have destruction." (Proverbs 13:3).

Sometimes, less conventional methods needed to be employed in order to correct orthodontic problems. Witness Solomon's observation: "In the mouth of the foolish is a rod." (Proverbs 14:3).

When we have broken-down teeth, we may find comfort in the reassurance that, at the very least, "the prudent are crowned." (Proverbs 14:18).

Mordecai acknowledged that quality dentisty can be a sound investment. He wrote that in "the crown of the wise is their riches." (Proverbs 14:24).

Today,
we know
that bacteria
on the tongue
can be the source
of bad breath. But even
among ancient Israelites,
it was understood that
"a wholesome tongue
is a tree of life."
(Proverbs 15:4).

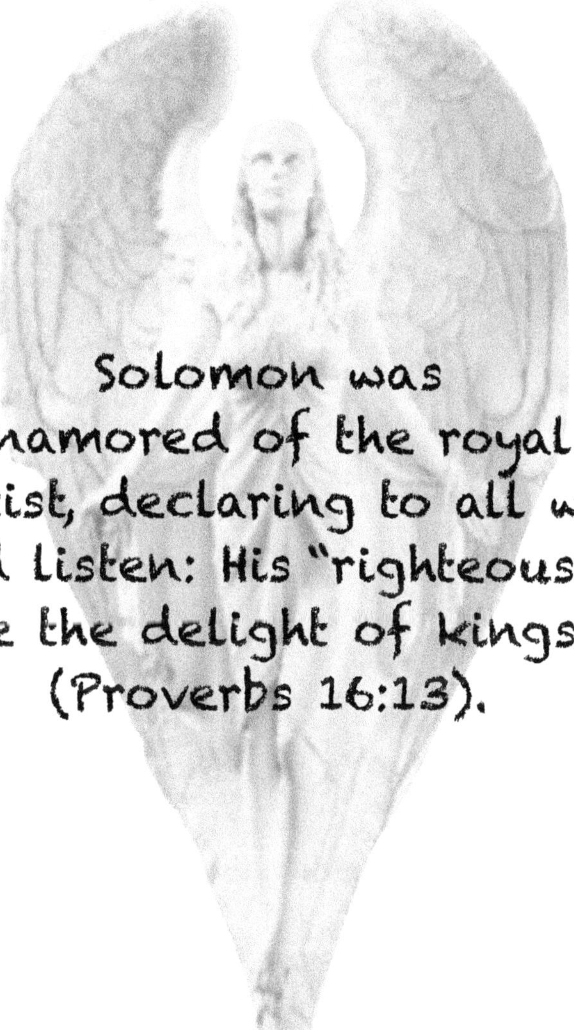

Solomon was
enamored of the royal
dentist, declaring to all who
would listen: His "righteous lips
are the delight of kings."
(Proverbs 16:13).

Too much exposure to the intense ultraviolet radiation of the desert sun put Israelites at risk of developing a cold sore. Of one of his subjects, Solomon reported: "In his lips there is as a burning fire." (Proverbs 16:27).

Solomon emphatically condemned the results of Botox therapy, declaring: "A wicked doer giveth heed to false lips." (Proverbs 17:4).

In
ancient
Israel, those
who neglected
oral hygiene and
regular professional
care were short-sighted.
As Solomon counseled his
people: "A fool's mouth is
his destruction, and his
lips are the snare."
(Proverbs 18:7).

One Israelite dentist wrote in his chart notations that, after using Restalin on a patient, "with the increase of his lips shall he be filled." (Proverbs 18:20).

In ancient Israel, one visionary dentist recognized the relationshp of oral hygene to mischief, and reported: "Whoso keepeth his mouth and his tongue, keepeth his soul from trouble." (Proverbs 21:23).

Where in all of Israel could a good dentist be found? "Confidence in an unfaithful man in time of trouble is like a broken tooth," wrote Solomon. (Proverbs 25:19).

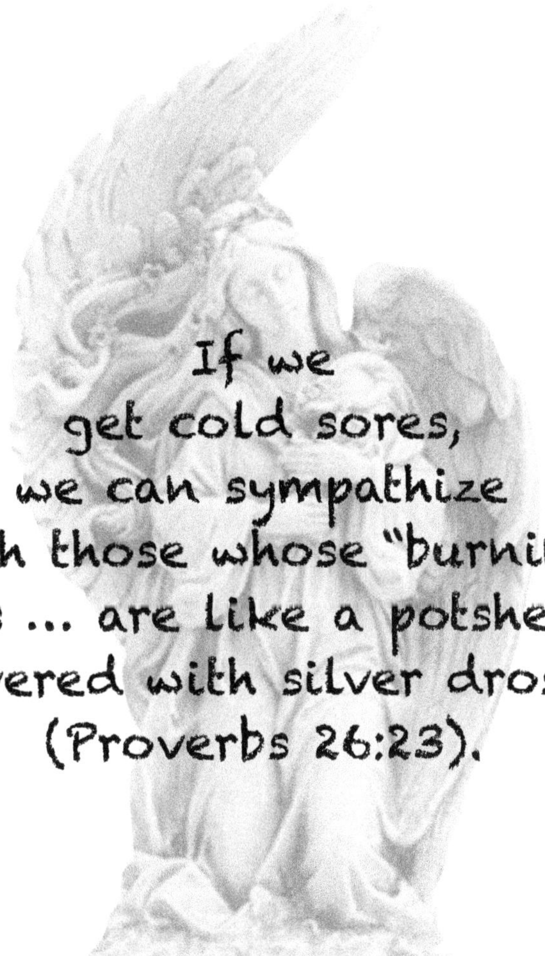

If we
get cold sores,
we can sympathize
with those whose "burning
lips ... are like a potsherd
covered with silver dross."
(Proverbs 26:23).

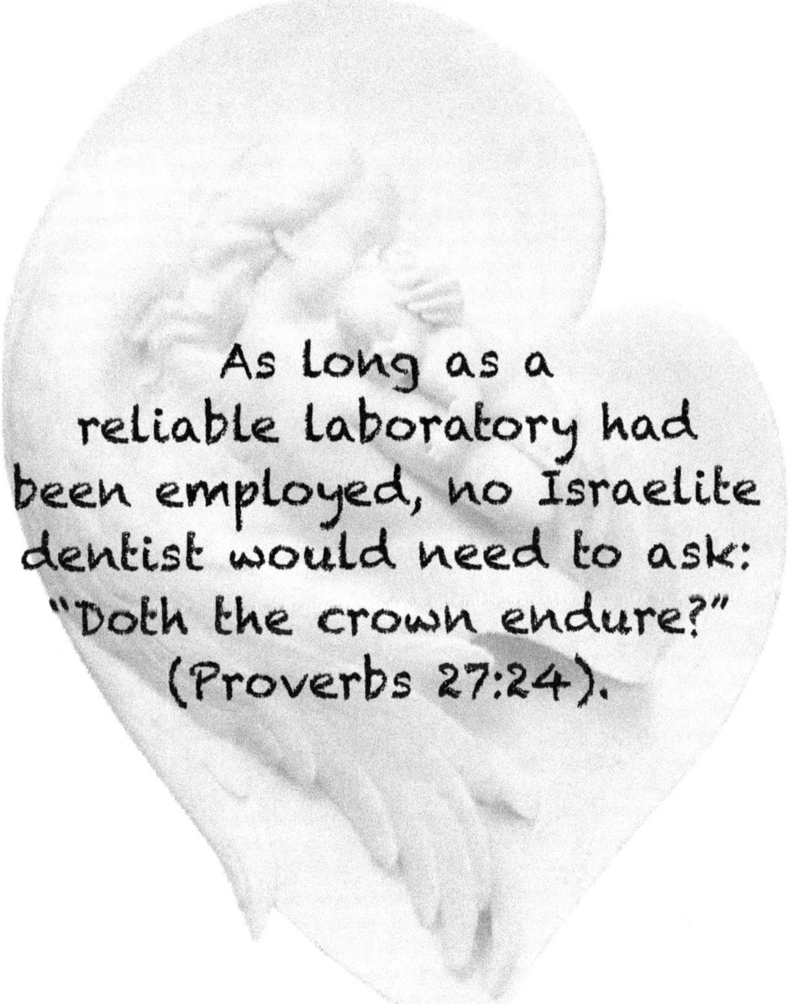

As long as a
reliable laboratory had
been employed, no Israelite
dentist would need to ask:
"Doth the crown endure?"
(Proverbs 27:24).

It is reported in
the Old Testament that
dentists sometimes acted
out their aggression on their
hapless patients. In the Book
of Proverbs, we read about
a "generation whose teeth
are as swords, and their
jaw teeth as knives."
(Proverbs 30:14).

Without Food and Drug Administration oversight, quality control of medicaments was dreadful. One investigative journalist reported: "Dead flies cause the ointment of the apothecary to send forth a stinking savour." (Ecclesiastes 10:1).

In Israel,
patients with rampant
caries sometimes required
full mouth restoration with
two full arches of sparklinhg
white porcelain crowns. Following
treatment, to one such indivdual,
Solmon gushed: "Thy cheeks are
comely, with rows of jewels."
(Song of Solomon 1:10).

To one happy patient who had just completed her treatment, an orthodontist in Jerusalem proudly exclaimed: "Thy teeth are like a flock of sheep that are even-shorn." (Song of Solomon 4:2).

It is a little-
known fact that in Old
Testament times, much attention
was focused on permanent make-up.
Solomon complimented one discretely
tattoed Israelite woman: "Thy lips
are like a thread of scarlet."
(Song of Solomon 4:3).

King Solomon
knew when his people
had done a poor job brushing
their teeth. After one surprise oral
exam, he could not stop himself
from blurting out: "Honey and
milk are under thy tongue."
(Song of Solomon 4:11).

The successful completion
of a treatment plan could leave a
dentist with feelings of exhilaration.
One made chart notations of a patient
whose "cheeks (were) as a bed of spices,
as sweet flowers: his lips like lilies,
dropping sweet smelling myrrh."
(Song of Solomon 5:13).

One
did not need
to be a dentist to be
able to predict that, should
oral health care be neglected,
it would very soon "come to pass
that instead of sweet smell,
there shall be stink."
(Isaiah 3:24).

Isaiah used
a drill without
water coolant, to the
end that, not only the
treatment room, but also
the entire "house was
filled with smoke."
(Isaiah 6:4).

Isaiah knew that the surfaces of the teeth were not the only areas upon which one should focus oral hygiene attention. He lamented: "Woe is me, for I am undone, because I am a man of unclean lips." (Isaiah 6:5).

Cavities in the front teeth could be very unesthetic. Writing about just such a stuation, Isaiah exclaimed: "Lo, this hath touched thy lips." (Isaiah 6:7).

One desperate wife in Israel called the dental office to complain of her husband: "With the breath of his lips, shall he slay the wicked." (Isaiah 11:4).

Witness the observation made by an Israelite speech therapist: "With stammering lips and another tongue, will he speak to this people." (Isaiah 28:11).

Once, in Israel,
a neighbor's halitosis was
so bad that friends worried:
"His breath, as an overflowing
stream, shall reach to the
midst of the neck."
(Isaiah 30:28).

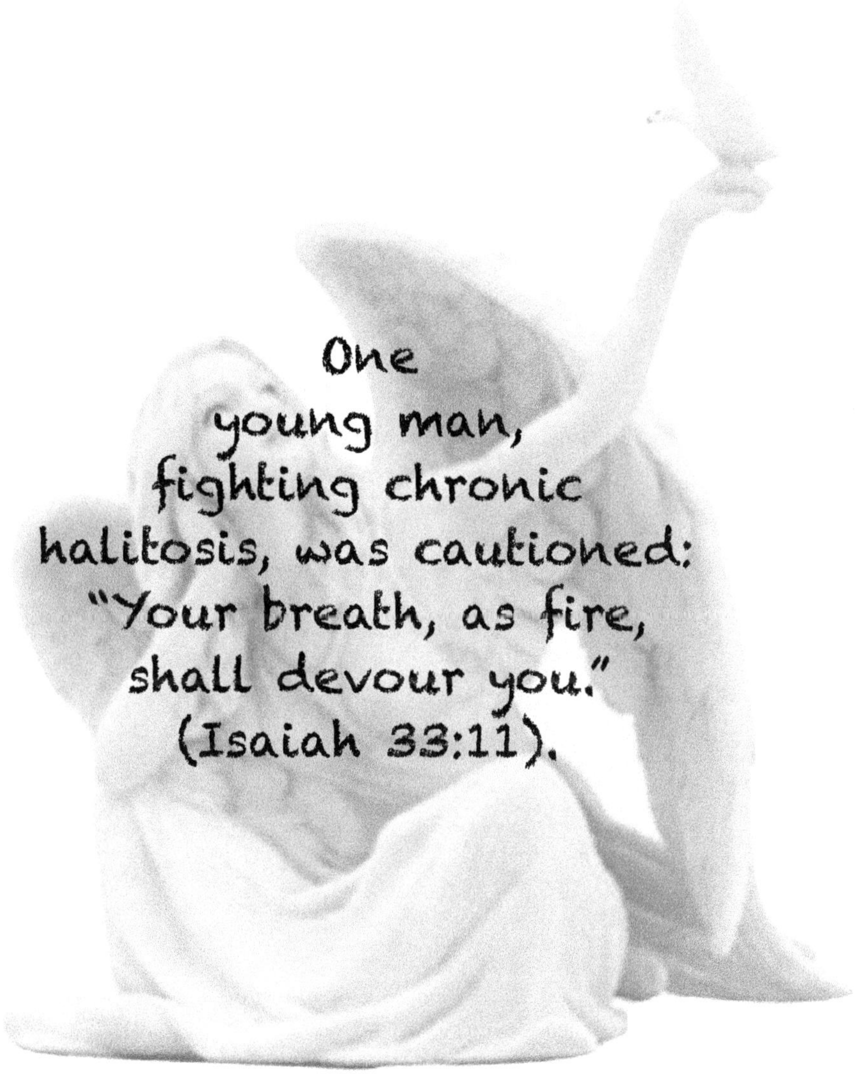

One
young man,
fighting chronic
halitosis, was cautioned:
"Your breath, as fire,
shall devour you."
(Isaiah 33:11).

Some of us can relate to the unhygienic experience of using a cuspidor. In ancient Israel, Isaiah admitted: "I hid not my face from shame and spitting." (Isaiah 50:6).

Sometimes, we are so terrified when we visit the dentist, that we are uncooperative, and even unresponsive. "He was afflicted, yet he opened not his mouth," reported Isaiah of one such individual. (Isaiah 53:7).

Once, a distraught mother telephoned a pedatric dentist's office to report an emergency, explaining to the staff member who answered the phone how "the children of Noph and Tahapanes have broken the crown." (Jeremiah 2:16).

One dentist with a large Jerusalem practice had a reputation for placing restorations in the teeth of one and all. His ultimate goal, it seemed, was to "fill all the inhabitants of this land." (Jeremiah 13:13).

Orthodontic treatment was available in Israel, for as Jeremiah reported: all "the children's teeth are set on edge." (Jeremiah 31:29).

One dentist who determined to have an "amalgam-free" practice, endured the wrath of her colleagues, who were perversely proud of their own mercury fillings. The local peer review board informed her: "All thine enemies have opened their mouth against thee." (Lamentations 2:16).

Biting down unawares on even small grains of sand can have dire consequences. How ironic that it is in the Book of Lamentations, of all places, that we read: "He hath also broken my teeth with gravel stone." (Lamentations 3:16).

When
seeking oral health
care, it is important to
follow the instructions of
the staff. At the commencement
of an appointment, one dentist in
Israel is reported to have said:
"When I speak with thee, I
will open thy mouth."
(Ezekiel 3:27).

When parents are anxious, their stress is sometimes manifest in the behavior of their offspring. "The fathers," the prophet Ezekiel wrote, "have eaten sour grapes, and the children's teeth are set on edge." (Ezekiel 18:2).

Old Testament dentists understood that the excessve use of facial cosmetics could be bad for your health. Thus, we read the counsel of the prophet Ezekel: "Ye shall not cover your lips." (Ezekiel 24:22).

Oral surgery was a specialty procedure to be attempted only by the most skilled of the dental practitioner prophets. "I will put hooks in thy jaws" for fixed intro-osseous retention, wrote Ezekiel. (Ezekiel 29:4).

You should be true to your teeth, or they will be false to you. In Israel, a dentist said of several of his patients: "With their mouth they shew much love, but their heart goeth after their covetousness." (Ezekiel 33:31).

In a vision,
Daniel beheld a
reception room that
was full of scary patients,
including a "beast (who) had
great iron teeth" reminiscent
of non-precious crowns.
(Daniel 7:7).

To Israel, Hosea compared himself to dentists who used mouth props. "I was to them as they that take off the yoke on their jaws," said the prophet. (Hosea 11:4).

Sometimes,
Israelite prosthodontists
didn't get the tooth mould
right when fitting full dentures.
One described a vast multitude of
patients who had come up upon
his "land, strong, and without
number, whose teeth are
the teeth of a lion."
(Joel 1:6).

Many don't realize dental hygienists were actively practicing in the Holy Land thousands of years ago. The Lord reported through Amos: "I also have given you cleanness of teeth in all your cities." (Amos 4:6). Rural areas, however, experienced a personnel shortage.

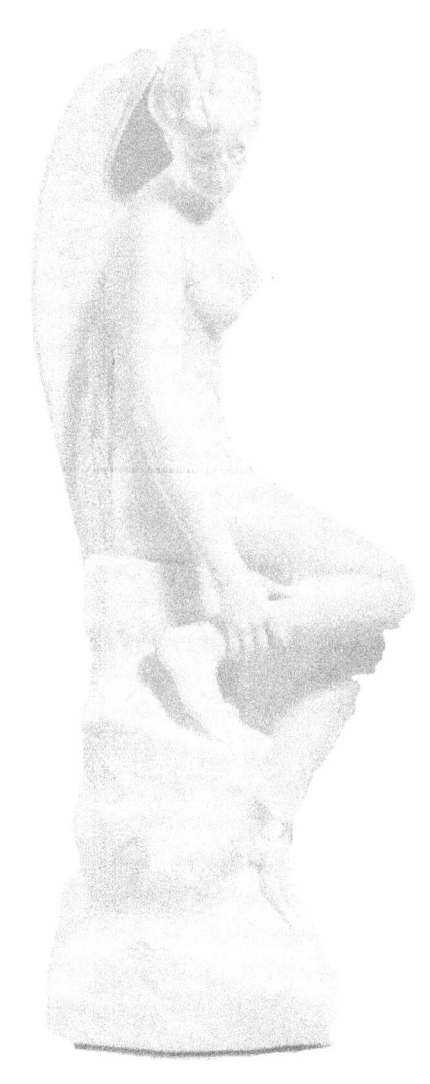

"Thus saith the Lord concerning the prophets (or dentists) that make my people err, that bite with their teeth." (Micah 3:5).

Dental lab technicians in ancient Israel observed the same methods as their mondern-day counterparts. All they had to do was to "take silver and gold, and make crowns." (Zechariah 6:11).

One confident Israelite periodontist declared: "I will take away his blood out of his mouth, and his abominations from between his teeth." (Zechariah 9:7).

The cuspidor came in handy on occasion, even for the Savior, Who "spit, and touched his tongue." (Matthew 7:33).

The immediate results of soft tissue surgery were sometimes spectacular. Of one patient, Matthew reported: "And straightway ... the string of his tongue was loosed, and he spake plain." (Matthew 7:35).

The Savior foresaw our day, when tensions would run high. "There shall be wailing and gnashing of teeth," He prophesied. (Matthew 13:42).

Nausea was a problem to be dealt with, even then. The Savor taught His disciples: "That which cometh out of the mouth, this defileth a man." (Matthew 15:11).

The scenario that was played out in one Israelite practice is all too familiar. It was reported that one of the dentist's patients actually "spit in his face." (Matthew 26:67).

Patients can become unexpectedly aggressive. One who suddenly turned on his dentist, "spit on his eyes, and put his hands upon him." (Mark 8:23).

Mark wrote
of one patient,
who, in consequence
of the overzealous use of
oral irrigation, "foameth, and
gnasheth with his teeth."
(Mark 9:18).

Following
the surgcal release
of a muscle attachment
on several of her patients,
one Israelite dentist declared
with satisfaction: "They shall
speak with new tongues."
(Mark 16:17).

The judicious use of a rubber dam to create a barrier between the teeth and the throat creates an environment, that was descrbed by the Apostle Paul, in which the aspiration of debris in "every mouth may be stopped."
(Romans 3:19).

It was sound advice to maintain oral hygiene followng the placement of fixed prosthetics. "Hold that fast which thou hast," the Apostle John cautioned, "that no man take thy crown." (Revelation 3:11).

Most of the time, fixed prostheses were fabricated in a dental laboratory. In one such facility, in order to meet the demands of dentists, "four and twenty elders ... cast their crowns." (Revelation 4:10).

Today,
fewer equestrians
visit the dentist, probably
because of parking concerns.
"And I saw, and behold a white
horse, and he that sat on him
had a bow; and a crown
was given unto him."
(Revelation 6:2).

Those in ancent
Israel who had inflamed
papillas on their tongues found the
discomfort to be such a distraction that
John was horrified to report that "they
gnawed their tongues for pain."
(Revelation 30:10).

Every dentist
philosophically accepts
the occupational hazard that
was endured by the Lord. In His
day, as in our own, thoughtless
patients "spit upon him,
and he suffereth it."
(1 Nephi 19:9).

Moses evidently had a tongue tie that was not addressed by surgery, for the Lord said of him: "Yet I will not loose his tongue, that he shall speak much." (2 Nephi 3:17).

With efficient mastication in mind, dentists paid attention to anatomical detail when creating restorations. Following treatment, one happy patient exclaimed: "He hath made my mouth like a sharp sword." (1 Nephi 21:2).

There were times
when the outcome of a
soft tissue surgical procedure
was beyond the control of even the
most faithful Israelite dentists. On
one occasion, it was revealed
that "the Lord shall utterly
destroy the tongue."
(2 Nephi 21:15).

Abinadi reported that anxiety can precipitate a variety of jaw-related problems. He said those who don't seek immediate attention "shall have cause to howl, and weep, and wail, and gnash their teeth." (Mosiah 16:2).

In a bustling downtown Zarahemla dental practice that was not known for a friendly chairside manner, it was quite understandable that all its patients would be "filled with pain and anguish." (Mosiah 25:11).

In Ammonihah, the preaching of Alma and Amulek exerted a negative effect upon its citizens, who started "gnashing their teeth upon them, and spitting upon them." (Alma 14:21).

In a practice in the Land of Bountiful, following the administration of local anesthetic, Mormon was moved to observe: "And no tongue can speak." (3 Nephi 17:17).

Many patients had breakfast before scheduling their early morning appointments. In the end, "they had eaten and (only then, their teeth) were filled." (3 Nephi 18:4).

Sometimes, a simple tongue tie release can make a huge difference. Of one particularly skilled dentist in Zarahemla, Mormon reported: "He loosed their tongues, that they could utter." (3 Nephi 26:14).

Mormon acompanied a friend who had just left the dental office. "And it is impossible for the tongue to describe" how elated he was to have his appointment behind him. (Mormon 4:11).

A Nephite dentist who had pioneered innovatve soft tissue procedures promised that, post-surgically, his patients would be able to "speak with new tongues." (Mormon 9:24).

Soon after the Restoration of the Gospel, members of the Church learned about the relationship between soft tissue oral surgical procedures and faithful obedience. Hence, the Saints were counseled: "First seek to obtain my word, and then shall your tongue be loosed." (D&C 11:21).

Suturing can
inhibit mobility, which is
not such a bad thing when
a patient is prone to criticize
the treatment they have received.
Following his zealous use of catgut,
one dentist in Fayette declared with
satisfaction: "Their tongues shall
be stayed, that they shall
not utter against me."
(D&C 29:19).

In Fayette, New York, in 1830, a critical need for oral health care prompted one dentist to promise prospective patients in the community: "Open your mouths and they shall be filled." (D&C 33:8).

Top quality
oral health care can
be expensive. The dental
society in Fayette, New York,
lobbied the local population to
dig deep into their pockets.
They urged every family:
"Open your mouths
and spare not."
(D&C 33:9).

Speaking of those who could not at the present time afford state of the art oral health care, the Savior promised: "They shall receive a crown in the mansions of my Father." (D&C 59:2).

A smoothly running dental practice requires the cooperation of its patients. One dentist privately complained to a colleague: "With some, I am not well pleased, for they will not open their mouths." (D&C 60:2).

There were times when a procedure seemed to good to be true. To those skeptics, one dentist gave the following instruction: "Let the unbelieving hold their lips." (D&C 63:6). He knew that when the time was right, they would follow his recommended treatment.

Joseph Smith asked God if he might be permitted to partake of sticky foods, like gum drops. He was reassured that, were he to do so, he would "in nowise lose his crown." (D&C 75:28).

Those who are not valiant in the testimony of Jesus "obtain not the crown." (D&C 76:79). They have to learn to make do with large silver fillings.

Faithful Latter-day Saints have been exhorted: "Come up unto the crown prepared for you." (D&C 78:15).

Frequently, even in the absence of dental insurance coverage, "the saints arose, and were crowned." (Moses 7:56).

Author's Note

And so, here we have it. One hundred twenty five examples of references to dentstry in the scriptures. Who would have guessed? Indeed, God certainly moves in mysterious ways.

"God moves in a mysterious way, His wonders to perform. He plants His footsteps in the sea, and rides upon the storm.

Deep in unfathomable mines of never failing skill, He treasures up His bright designs, and works His sovereign will.

Ye fearful saints, fresh courage take. The clouds ye so much dread are big with mercy, and shall break in blessings on your head.

Judge not
the Lord by feeble
sense, but trust Him for His
grace. Behind a frowning
providence He hides
a smiling face.

His purposes will
ripen fast, unfolding
every hour. The bud
may have a bitter
taste, but sweet
will be the
flower.

Unbelief is sure to err, and scan His work in vain. God is His own interpreter, and He will make it plain."

"God Moves
in a Mysterious Way"
(William Cowper - 1773).

Appendix One

Chronological references to dentistry in the scriptures, as they appear in the text of the volume.

Genesis 49:12
Exodus 4:10
Exodus 4:11
Exodus 16:12
Exodus 21:24
Exodus 37:2
Leviticus 35:14
Numbers 11:33
Judges 15:191
1 Samuel 1:13
1 Samuel 2:13
2 Samuel 22:9 & 16
Esther 8:15
Job 5:21
Job 6:30
Job 13:14
Job 16:5
Job 16:9
Job 17:1
Job 19:7
Job 19:17
Job 29:10
Job 29:17
Job 41:2
Job 41:14
Psalms 3:7
Psalms 12:3

Psalms 12:4
Psalms 22:15
Psalms 35:16
Psalms 39:1
Psalms 57:4
Psalms 58:6
Psalms 59:7
Psalms 89:39
Psalms 115:5
Psalms 140:3
Proverbs 5:3
Proverbs 10:14
Proverbs 10:26
Proverbs 10:31
Proverbs 13:3
Proverbs 14:3
Proverbs 14:18
Proverbs 14:24
Proverbs 15:4
Proverbs 16:3
Proverbs 16:13
Proverbs 16:27
Proverbs 17:4
Proverbs 18:7
Proverbs 18:20
Proverbs 21:23
Proverbs 25:19

Proverbs 26:23
Proverbs 27:24
Proverbs 30:14
Ecclesiastes 10:1
Song of Solomon 1:10
Song of Solomon 4:2
Song of Solomon 4:3
Song of Solomon 4:11
Song of Solomon 5:13
Isaiah 3:24
Isaiah 6:4
Isaiah 6:5
Isaiah 6:7
Isaiah 11:4
Isaiah 28:11
Isaiah 30:28
Isaiah 33:11
Isaiah 50:6
Isaiah 53:7
Jeremiah 2:16
Jeremiah 13:13
Jeremiah 31:29
Lamentations 2:16
Lamentations 3:16
Ezekiel 3:27

Ezekiel 18:2
Ezekiel 24:22
Ezekiel 29:4
Ezekiel 33:31
Daniel 7:7
Hosea 11:4
Joel 1:6
Amos 4:6
Micah 3:5
Zechariah 6:11
Zechariah 9:7

Matthew 7:33
Matthew 7:35
Matthew 13:42
Matthew 15:11
Matthew 26:67
Mark 8:23
Mark 9:18
Mark 16:17
Romans 3:19
Revelation 3:11
Revelation 4:10
Revelation 6:2
Revelation 30:10

1 Nephi 19:9
1 Nephi 21:2
2 Nephi 3:17
2 Nephi 21:15
Mosiah 16:2
Mosiah 25:11
Alma 14:21
3 Nephi 17:17
3 Nephi 18:4
3 Nephi 26:14
Mormon 4:11
Mormon 9:24

D&C 11:21
D&C 29:19
D&C 33:8
D&C 33:9
D&C 59:2
D&C 63:6
D&C 75:28
D&C 76:79
D&C 78:15

Moses 7:56

About The Author

Phil Hudson and his wife Jan have 7 children and over 25 grandchildren. They enjoy spending time with their family at their cabin nestled in the Selkirk Mountains, on the shore of Priest Lake, the crown jewel of North Idaho. Phil had a successful dental practice in Spokane, Washington for 43 years, before retiring in 2015. He has an eclectic mix of hobbies, and enjoys the out of doors. He always finds time, however, to record his thoughts on his laptop, and understands Isaac Asimov's response when he was asked: If you knew that you had only 10 minutes left to live, what would you do?" He answered: "I'd type faster."

Phil received the inspiration to write this book while he and Jan were serving as missionaries for The Church of Jesus Christ of Latter-day Saints, in the Kingdom of Tonga. While there, they celebrated their 50th wedding anniversary.

By The Author

Essays

    Volume One: Spray From The Ocean Of Thought
    Volume Two: Ripples On A Pond
    Volume Three: Serendipitous Meanderings
    Volume Four: Presents Of Mind
    Volume Five: Mental Floss
    Volume Six: Fitness Training For The Mind And Spirit

First Principles and Ordinances Series

    Faith – Our Hearts Are Changed
    Repentance – A Broken Heart and a Contrite Spirit
    Baptism – One Hundred And One Reasons Why We Are Baptized
    The Holy Ghost – That We Might Have His Spirit To Be With Us
    The Sacrament – This Do In Remembrance Of Me

Book of Mormon Commentary

    Volume One: Born In The Wilderness
    Volume Two: Voices From The Dust
    Volume Three: Journey To Cumorah

Doctrine & Covenants Commentary

    Volume One - Sections 1 - 34
    Volume Two - Sections 35 - 57

Minute Musings: Spontaneous Combustions of Thought

    Volume One
    Volume Two
    Volume Three

Calendars:

    As I Think About The Savior
    In His Own Words: Discovering William Tyndale
    Scriptural Symbols

Children & Youth

    Book of Mormon Hiking Song
    Happy Birthday
    Muddy, Muddy
    The Hiawatha Trail: An Allegory
    The Little Princess
    The Parable of The Pencil
    The Thirteen Articles of Faith

Doctrinal Themes

    Are Christians Mormon? Volume One
    Are Christians Mormon? Volume One
    Christmas is The Season When...
    Dentistry in The Scriptures
    Gratitude
    Hebrew Poetry
    Hiding in Plain Sight
    One Hundred Questions Answered by The Book of Mormon
    The Highways and Byways of Life
    The House of The Lord
    The Parable of The Pencil
    Without The Book of Mormon
    Writing on Metal Plates

A Thought For Each Day of the Year

    Baptism
    Faith
    Life's Greatest Questions
    Repentance
    Revelation
    The Atonement
    The Holy Ghost
    The House of the Lord
    The Plan of Salvation
    The Sabbath
    The Sacrament

Professional Publications

    Diode Laser Soft Tissue Surgery Volume One
    Diode Laser Soft Tissue Surgery Volume Two
    Diode Laser Soft Tissue Surgery Volume Three

These, and other titles, are available from online retailers.

Quid magis possum dicere?

www.ingramcontent.com/pod-product-compliance
Lightning Source LLC
Chambersburg PA
CBHW060507240426
43661CB00007B/942